Success With

Math

SCHOLASTIC

Editor: Ourania Papacharalambous
Cover design by Tannaz Fassihi; cover illustration by Kevin Zimmer
Interior design by Cynthia Ng
Interior illustrations by Stephen Brown (19, 24–25, 29); Doug Jones (spot art); Cynthia Ng (14, 26, 28, 30)

ISBN 978-1-338-79848-7
Scholastic Inc., 557 Broadway, New York, NY 10012
Copyright © 2022 Scholastic Inc.
All rights reserved. Printed in the U.S.A.
First printing, January 2022
1 2 3 4 5 6 7 8 9 10   40 29 28 27 26 25 24 23 22

INTRODUCTION

Parents and teachers alike will find *Scholastic Success With Math* to be a valuable educational tool. It is designed to help students in the first grade improve their math skills. The practice pages incorporate challenging puzzles, inviting games, and picture problems that children are sure to enjoy. On page 4, you will find a list of the key skills covered in the activities throughout this book. Children will practice recognizing shapes and patterns, reading charts and graphs, solving problems, and performing basic computations. They are also challenged to measure length, width, and volume, identify fractions, and tell time. Remember to praise children for their efforts and successes!

TABLE OF CONTENTS

Grade-Appropriate Skills Covered in *Scholastic Success With Math: Grade 1*

Apply properties of operations as strategies to add and subtract.

Understand subtraction as an unknown-addend problem. For example, subtract 10 - 8 by finding the number that makes 10 when added to 8.

Relate counting to addition and subtraction.

Add and subtract within 20, demonstrating fluency for addition and subtraction within 10.

Understand that the two digits of a two-digit number represent amounts of tens and ones.

Understand that 10 can be thought of as a bundle of ten ones—called a "ten."

Understand that the numbers from 11 to 19 are composed of a ten and one, two, three, four, five, six, seven, eight, or nine ones.

Add within 100, including adding a two-digit number and a one-digit number.

Measure lengths indirectly and by iterating length units.

Order three objects by length; compare the lengths of two objects indirectly by using a third object.

Express the length of an object as a whole number of length units, by laying multiple copies of a shorter object end to end; understand that the length measurement of an object is the number of same-size length units that span it with no gaps or overlaps.

Tell and write time in hours and half-hours using analog and digital clocks.

Organize, represent, and interpret data with up to three categories; ask and answer questions about the total number of data points, how many in each category, and how many more or less are in one category than in another.

Distinguish between defining attributes versus non-defining attributes; build and draw shapes to possess defining attributes.

Partition circles and rectangles into two and four equal shares, describe the shares using the words halves, fourths, and quarters, and use the phrases half of, fourth of, and quarter of. Describe the whole as two of, or four of the shares. Understand for these examples that decomposing into more equal shares creates smaller shares.

So Many Flowers!

Count. Circle groups of 10. Write the number of tens and ones.

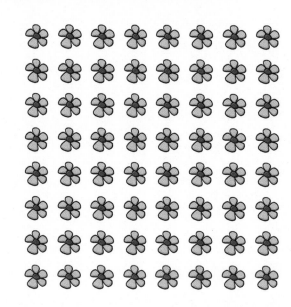

_____ tens   _____ ones   _____ tens   _____ ones

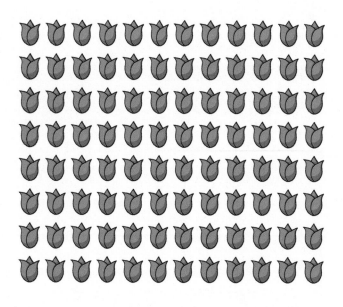

_____ tens   _____ ones   _____ tens   _____ ones

Have a Heart

Circle a group of 10. Write the number of tens and ones.

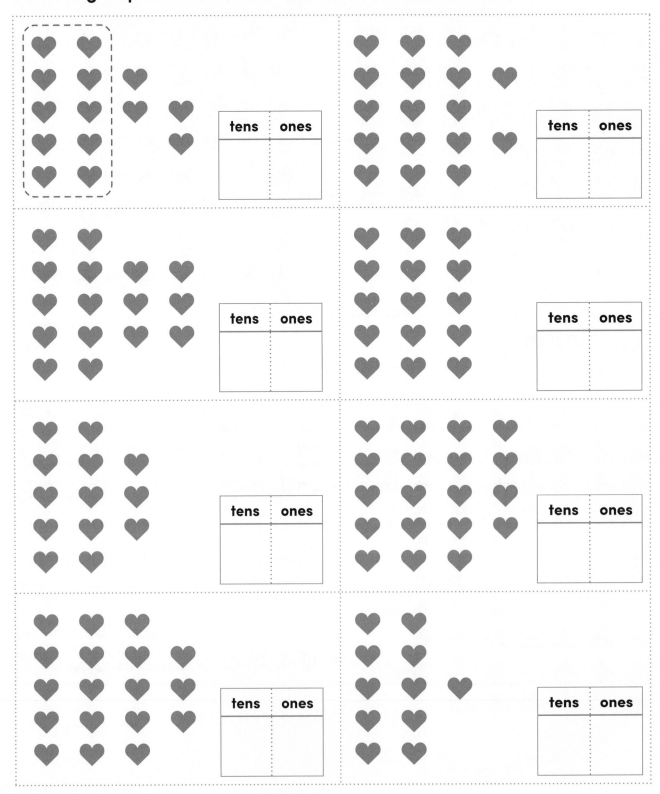

Sign Shape

Street signs come in different shapes. Use string to form the shapes below. Work with a partner. Answer the questions below about the shapes, too.

What shape is this sign? _____

How many sides does it have? _____

What shape is this sign? _____

How many sides does it have? _____

What shape is this sign? _____

How many sides does it have? _____

What shape is this sign? _____

How many sides does it have? _____

Bird Feeder Geometry

It's spring! The birds are coming back. Kwaku and his mother made two bird feeders.

What shapes can you find on their feeders? Write your ideas on the lines.

_____

_____

_____

Shape Study

Look at the pictures below. Color those that show symmetry. (Hint: Imagine the pictures are folded on the dotted lines.)

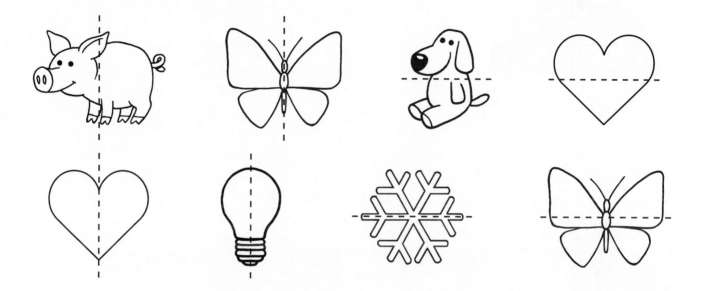

Complete the drawings below. Connect the dots to show the other half. (Hint: The pictures are symmetrical.)

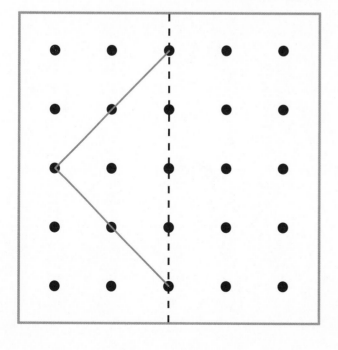
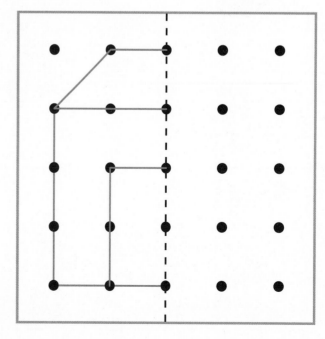

Give Us Symmetry!

Draw the other half of each shape.

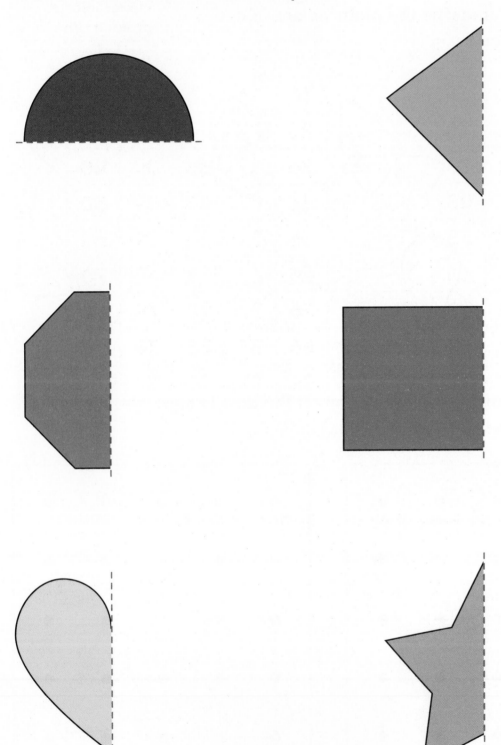

Picking Out Patterns

On the 100th day of school, everyone in Pat's class picked out patterns on the 100 Chart. Look at the chart below.

1	2	3	4	5	6	7	8	9	10
11	12	13	14	15	16	17	18	19	20
21	22	23	24	25	26	27	28	29	30
31	32	33	34	35	36	37	38	39	40
41	42	43	44	45	46	47	48	49	50
51	52	53	54	55	56	57	58	59	60
61	62	63	64	65	66	67	68	69	70
71	72	73	74	75	76	77	78	79	80
81	82	83	84	85	86	87	88	89	90
91	92	93	94	95	96	97	98	99	100

1 Find and finish the pattern starting with 2, 12, 22.

_____

2 Find and finish the pattern starting with 100, 90, 80.

_____

3 Find and finish the pattern starting with 97, 87, 77.

_____

4 Find and finish the pattern starting with 11, 22, 33.

_____

All Kinds of Patterns!

**Look at the patterns below.
Describe each pattern.
The first one is done for you.**

A **pattern** is something that repeats in a regular way. A pattern can include numbers, pictures, or shapes.

①

This is a pattern of three shapes, all the same color, that repeat.

②

_____

③

_____

④ **10   5   6   11   6   7   12   7   8   13   8   9**

_____

Create your own pattern in the space below.

Odd and Even Patterns

A pattern can have two things repeating. This is called an "AB" pattern.

1 Look around the room. What "AB" patterns do you see?
Draw one "AB" pattern in the box.

2 Use red and blue crayons to color the numbers
in the chart using an "AB" pattern.

Hundreds Chart

1	2	3	4	5	6	7	8	9	10
11	12	13	14	15	16	17	18	19	20
21	22	23	24	25	26	27	28	29	30
31	32	33	34	35	36	37	38	39	40
41	42	43	44	45	46	47	48	49	50
51	52	53	54	55	56	57	58	59	60
61	62	63	64	65	66	67	68	69	70
71	72	73	74	75	76	77	78	79	80
81	82	83	84	85	86	87	88	89	90
91	92	93	94	95	96	97	98	99	100

Use this rule:

1 = red

2 = blue

3 = red

4 = blue, and so on

The blue numbers are **even numbers**. They can be split evenly into 2 whole numbers.

The red numbers are **odd numbers**. They cannot be split evenly into 2 whole numbers.

Snowflakes on Mittens

Estimate how many snowflakes are on each mitten.
For the first mitten, skip count by 2s to find out.
(You can circle groups of two.)
For the second mitten, skip count by 5s to check your answer.
(You can circle groups of five.)

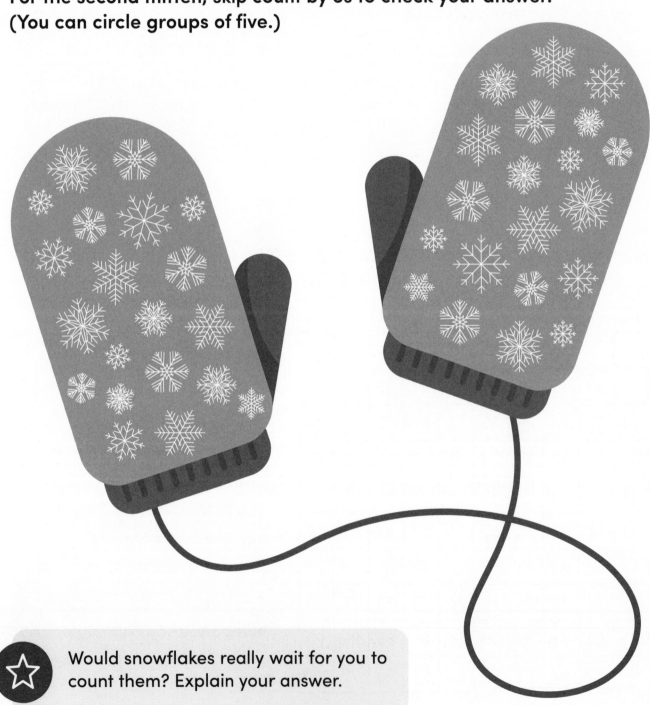

⭐ Would snowflakes really wait for you to count them? Explain your answer.

© Scholastic Inc.

Patterns of Five

Look at the number chart below. Starting with 1, count five squares. Color in the fifth space. Then count five more squares and color in the fifth square. Keep going until you reach 100.

Hundreds Chart

1	2	3	4	5	6	7	8	9	10
11	12	13	14	15	16	17	18	19	20
21	22	23	24	25	26	27	28	29	30
31	32	33	34	35	36	37	38	39	40
41	42	43	44	45	46	47	48	49	50
51	52	53	54	55	56	57	58	59	60
61	62	63	64	65	66	67	68	69	70
71	72	73	74	75	76	77	78	79	80
81	82	83	84	85	86	87	88	89	90
91	92	93	94	95	96	97	98	99	100

Tally marks can be arranged in groups of five, like this: |||| |||| ||||
Then you can count by fives.

Count how many girls you know. Draw tally marks in groups of five.

Girls: _____ Boys: _____

Now count the total number. Write the totals here:

Girls: _____ Boys: _____

Pattern Block Design

How many total pieces are in this pattern block design?

$$2 + 2 + 1 = \underline{\hspace{3cm}}$$

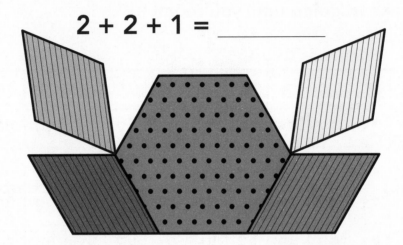

Now make your own design by drawing five pattern blocks. Connect the blocks to form a pattern different from the one above. You may want to use a block pattern more than once.

Write an equation to show how many of each shape you used.

Equation: _____

Snowflake Math

**Add. Color the picture.
Use the color key below.**

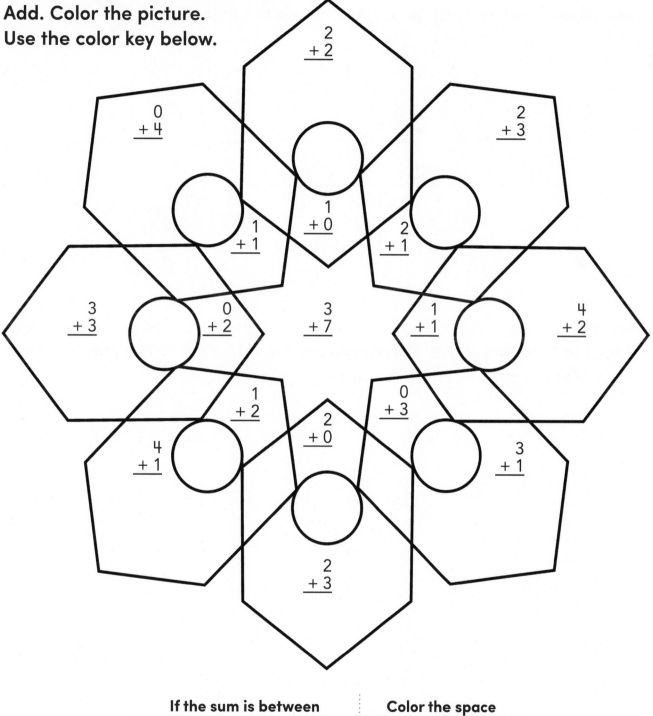

If the sum is between	Color the space
1 and 3	blue
4 and 6	purple
7 and 10	red

Fill in the other spaces with colors of your choice.

Key Code

Add. Then, use the code to answer the riddle below.

6 + 2	4 + 3	2 + 1	4 + 1
I	**D**	**H**	**A**
11 + 3	8 + 2	7 + 5	9 + 2
A	**B**	**N**	**S**
6 + 3	11 + 4	5 +13	9 + 4
O	**U**	**R**	**P**

What has 88 keys but can't open a single door?

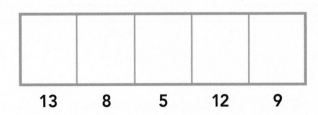

14   13   8   5   12   9

Where's the Beach?

Add. To find the path to the beach, color each box with an odd answer yellow.

	14 + 3	34 + 2	81 + 3	
76 + 2	25 + 4	56 + 3	11 + 3	40 + 8
87 + 1	22 + 2	32 + 3	65 + 1	93 + 5
10 + 8	41 + 2	70 + 7	32 + 6	84 + 4
73 + 5	63 + 2	55 + 1	41 + 5	23 + 3
	98 + 1	53 + 4	82 + 5	

By the Seashore

Use the code below to write each missing number. Add.

93
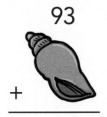
+ _____

82
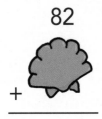
+ _____

14
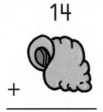
+ _____

21
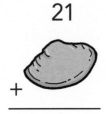
+ _____

53
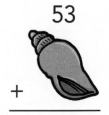
+ _____

45
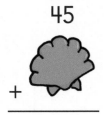
+ _____

73
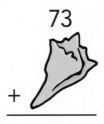
+ _____

36
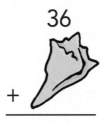
+ _____

61

+ _____

32
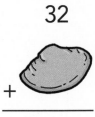
+ _____

Sunflower Math

Do the addition problems in the sunflower picture below.
Then, use the Color Key to color each answer.

Color Key

56	green
68	orange
89	yellow
97	blue

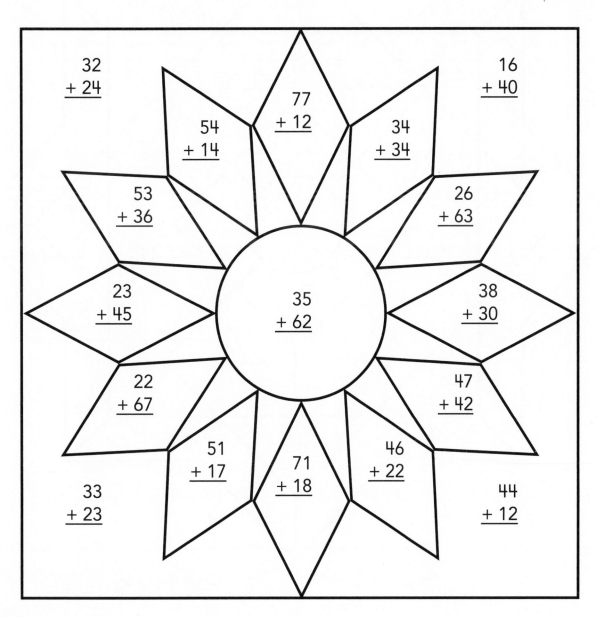

⭐ Write your age on four strips of paper. Then, add a 6, 7, 8, and 9 to your age on each strip of paper. Practice the answers with a friend.

Star Math

**Add. Color the picture.
Use the color key below.**

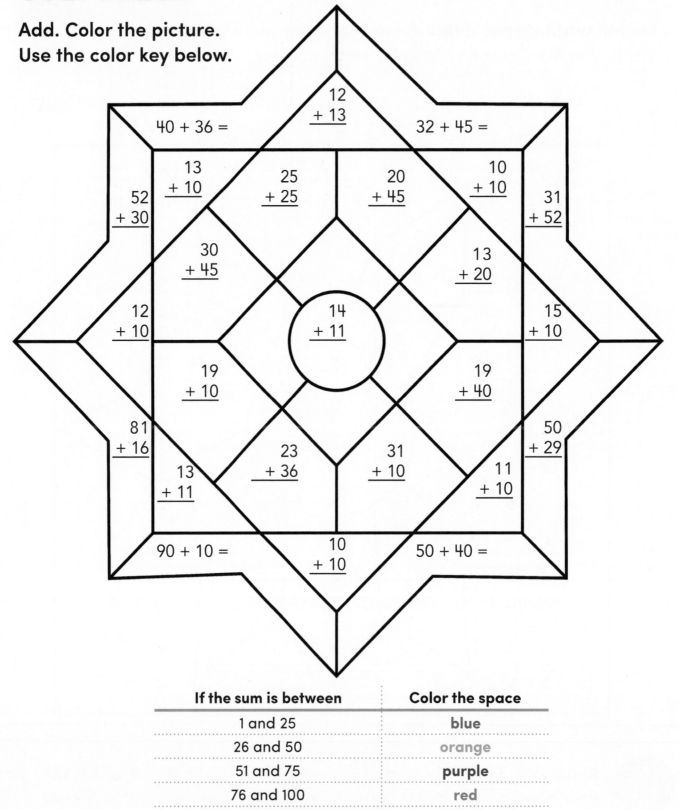

If the sum is between	Color the space
1 and 25	blue
26 and 50	orange
51 and 75	purple
76 and 100	red

Fill in the other spaces with colors of your choice.

The Big Search

Subtract. Circle the difference.

11 – 7 = five three (four)	14 – 9 = nine one five
13 – 6 = six nine seven	16 – 5 = twelve thirteen eleven
18 – 9 = eleven ten nine	17 – 11 = seven six ten
15 – 5 = ten seven five	12 – 9 = three two four
12 – 4 = six eight nine	11 – 9 = three five two

Find each circled number in the word puzzle. Look → and ↓.

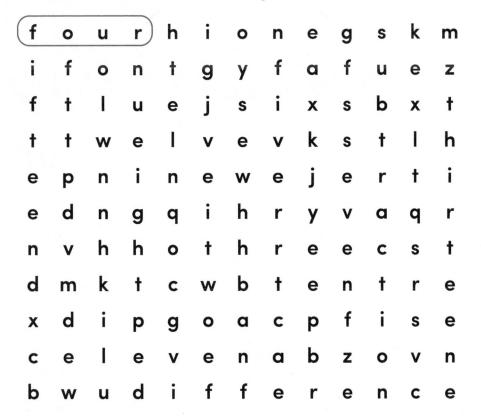

```
(f  o  u  r)  h  i  o  n  e  g  s  k  m
 i  f  o  n  t  g  y  f  a  f  u  e  z
 f  t  l  u  e  j  s  i  x  s  b  x  t
 t  t  w  e  l  v  e  v  k  s  t  l  h
 e  p  n  i  n  e  w  e  j  e  r  t  i
 e  d  n  g  q  i  h  r  y  v  a  q  r
 n  v  h  h  o  t  h  r  e  e  c  s  t
 d  m  k  t  c  w  b  t  e  n  t  r  e
 x  d  i  p  g  o  a  c  p  f  i  s  e
 c  e  l  e  v  e  n  a  b  z  o  v  n
 b  w  u  d  i  f  f  e  r  e  n  c  e
```

  See if you can find these number words: **twelve, fifteen, thirteen, subtraction, difference.**

Ocean Life

Use the math picture on the next page to count and write the number in each box. Subtract the numbers.

1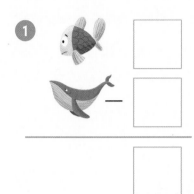

2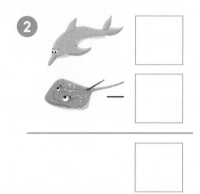

3

4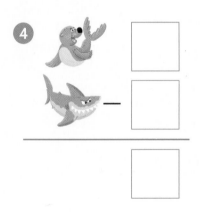

5

6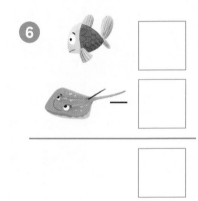

7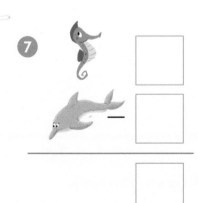

8

9

A Perfect Strike

Fill in the missing numbers to reach the sum on each ball.

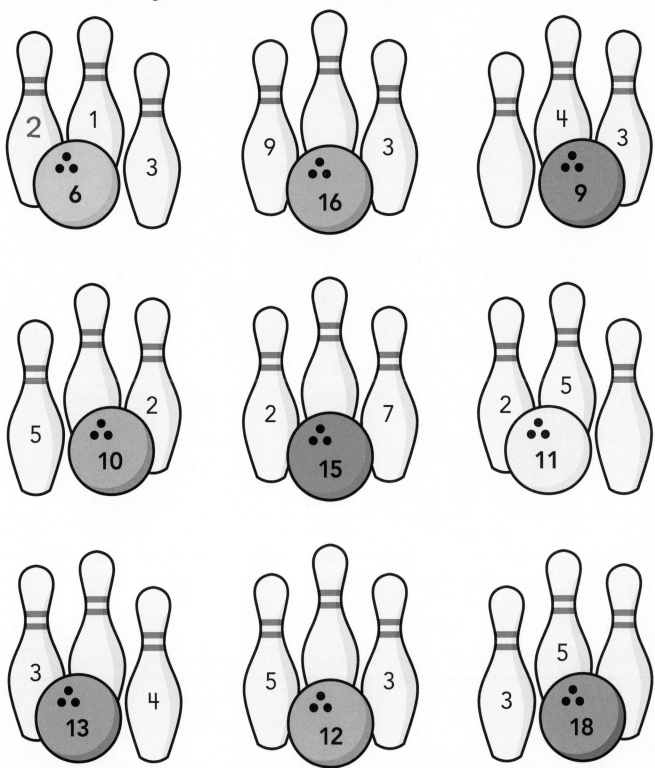

© Scholastic Inc.

How Much Money?

34¢ 21¢ 13¢ 52¢ 47¢ 10¢ 62¢ 75¢

Add to find out how much.

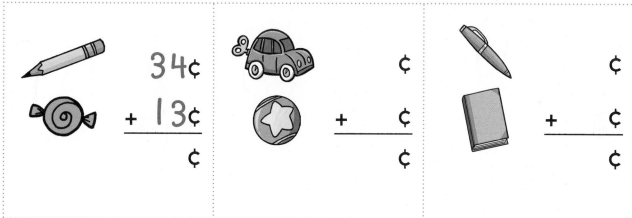

$$
\begin{array}{r}
34¢ \\
+\ 13¢ \\
\hline
¢
\end{array}
$$

$$
\begin{array}{r}
¢ \\
+\ ¢ \\
\hline
¢
\end{array}
$$

$$
\begin{array}{r}
¢ \\
+\ ¢ \\
\hline
¢
\end{array}
$$

Subtract to find out how much.

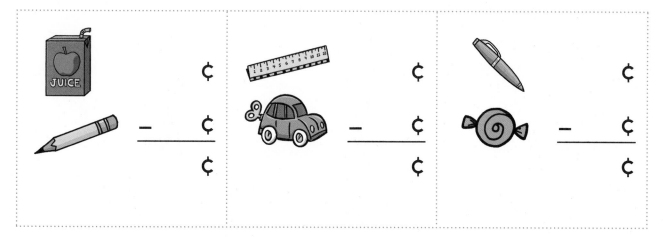

$$
\begin{array}{r}
¢ \\
-\ ¢ \\
\hline
¢
\end{array}
$$

$$
\begin{array}{r}
¢ \\
-\ ¢ \\
\hline
¢
\end{array}
$$

$$
\begin{array}{r}
¢ \\
-\ ¢ \\
\hline
¢
\end{array}
$$

Going to the Market

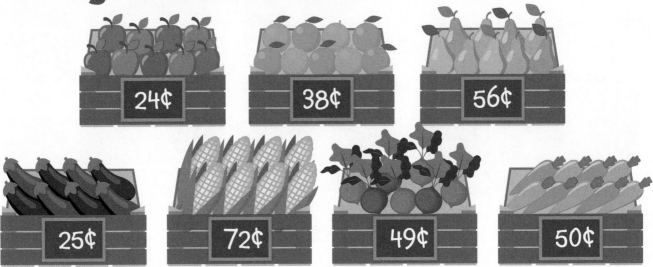

Add to find out how much.

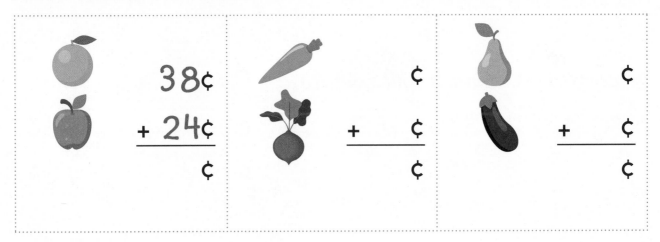

$$\begin{array}{r} 38¢ \\ + \ 24¢ \\ \hline ¢ \end{array}$$

Subtract to find out how much.

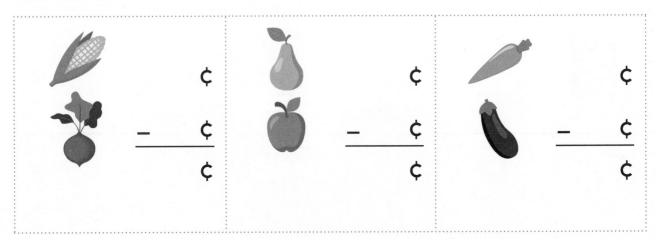

Measuring Up

**People didn't always measure with rulers.
Long ago, Egyptians and other people measured objects
with body parts. Try it!**

A "digit" is the width of your middle finger
at the top joint where it bends.

How many digits long is:

a pair of scissors? _____

a math book? _____

a crayon? _____

. . . .

A "palm" is the width of your palm.

How many palms long is:

a magazine? _____

your desk? _____

a ruler? _____

. . . .

A "span" is the length from the tip of your pinkie
to the tip of your thumb when your hand is wide open.

How many spans long is:

a broom handle? _____

a table? _____

a door? _____

Penguin Family on Parade

The penguin family is part of the winter parade. They need to line up from shortest to tallest. Give them a hand! Use a ruler to measure each penguin. Label each penguin with its height. Then write the name of each penguin in size order, from smallest to tallest.

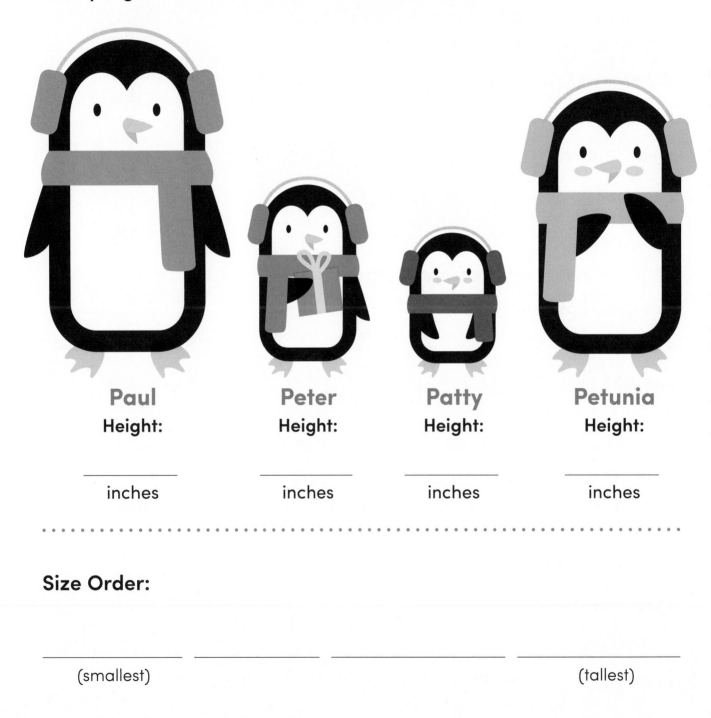

Paul	**Peter**	**Patty**	**Petunia**
Height:	Height:	Height:	Height:
_____	_____	_____	_____
inches	inches	inches	inches

Size Order:

_____ _____ _____ _____
(smallest)   (tallest)

Look and Learn

Look at each picture. Estimate how long you think it is. Then, measure each picture with a ruler. Write the actual length in inches.

Estimate: _____ inches

Actual: _____ inches

Estimate: _____ inches

Actual: _____ inches

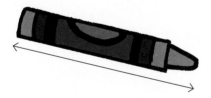

Estimate: _____ inches

Actual: _____ inches

Estimate: _____ inches

Actual: _____ inches

 Practice measuring other things in the room with a ruler.

Turn Up the Volume

How many quarts equal 1 gallon? Find out! Fill a quart container with water. Pour it into a gallon container. Keep doing it until the gallon is full. Color the correct number of quarts below.

Write the numeral on the line: **1 gallon =** _____ **quarts.**

Now try it with other containers.

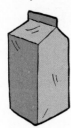    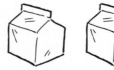

1 quart = _____ **pints**

1 pint = _____ **cups**

1 cup = _____ **tablespoons**

1 tablespoon = _____ **teaspoons**

Centimeters

Things can be measured using centimeters. Get a ruler that measures in centimeters. Measure the pictures of the objects below.

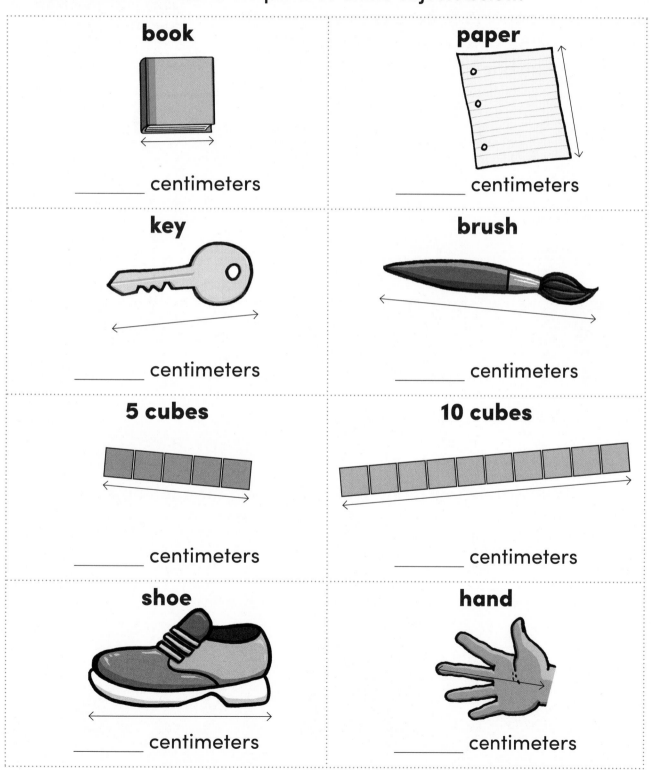

book

_____ centimeters

paper

_____ centimeters

key

_____ centimeters

brush

_____ centimeters

5 cubes

_____ centimeters

10 cubes

_____ centimeters

shoe

_____ centimeters

hand

_____ centimeters

Five Senses

Look at the pictures on the left side of the graph. Think about which of your senses you use to learn about it. Draw a check mark in the box to show the senses used. (Hint: You might use more than one.)

> We learn about the world by using our five senses. The five senses are seeing, hearing, smelling, touching, and tasting.

	See	Hear	Smell	Touch	Taste
(chicken)					
(sun)					
(milk)					
(flowers)					
(drum)					

Now graph how many senses you used for each object.

5					
4					
3					
2					
1					

(chicken) (sun) (milk) (flowers) (drum)

Rainbow Graph

Which color of the rainbow is your favorite? Color in the box for your favorite color. Have five friends color the boxes to show their favorite colors, too.

Which color is liked the most? _____

Which color is liked the least? _____

Are any colors tied? _____

Which ones? _____

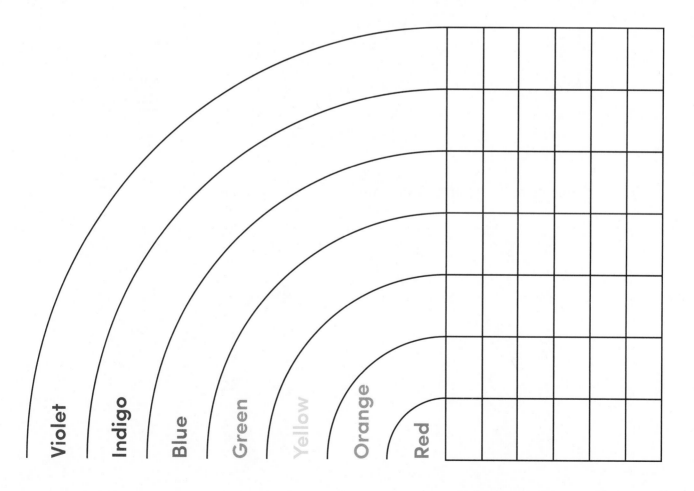

Violet Indigo Blue Green Yellow Orange Red

Fruits and Vegetables

Find the coordinates for each of the items in the grid.
The first one has been done for you.

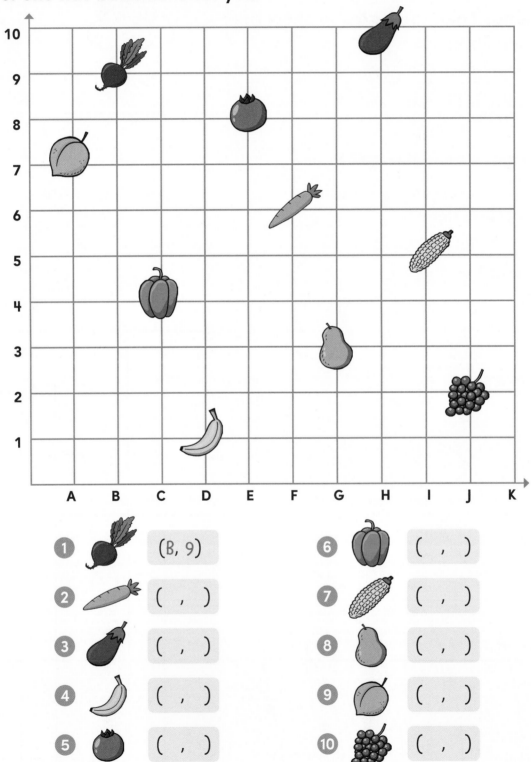

1 (B, 9)

2 (,)

3 (,)

4 (,)

5 (,)

6 (,)

7 (,)

8 (,)

9 (,)

10 (,)

Starry Night

Find each letter and number pair on the graph.
Draw a star for each. The first one has been done for you.

1 (F, 10)	4 (A, 4)	7 (I, 9)	10 (C, 1)
2 (G, 2)	5 (D, 8)	8 (K, 11)	11 (J, 5)
3 (B, 9)	6 (G, 6)	9 (D, 5)	12 (K, 2)

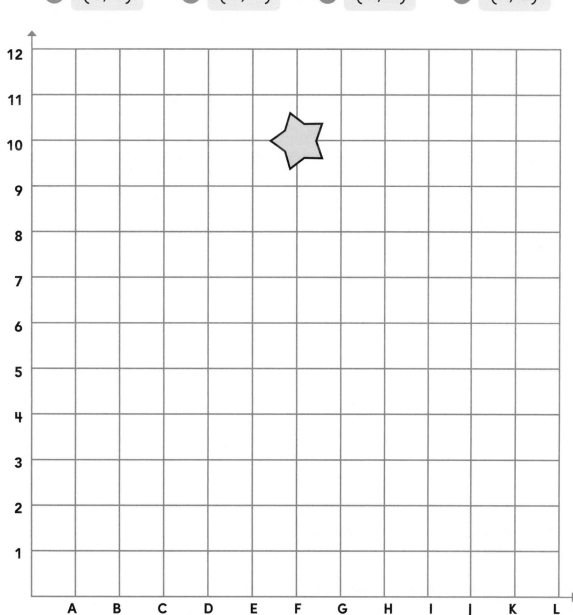

December Weather

In December, Mrs. Monroe's class drew the weather on a calendar. Each kind of weather has a picture:

sunny   cloudy   rainy   snowy

Look at the calendar. Answer the questions below.

December

SUN.	MON.	TUES.	WED.	THURS.	FRI.	SAT.
	1 ☁	2 ☁	3 ☀	4 ☁	5 💧	6 ❄
7 💧	8 ❄	9 ❄	10 ☀	11 ☀	12 ☁	13 ☀
14 ☁	15 ☀	16 ☀	17 ❄	18 ☀	19 ☁	20 💧
21 💧	22 ☁	23 ☀	24 ☀	25 💧	26 ❄	27 ☀
28 ❄	29 ☁	30 ☀	31 ☀			

How many sunny days did they have? _____

How many cloudy days did they have? _____

How many rainy days did they have? _____

How many snowy days did they have? _____

Which kind of weather did they have the most? _____

Fun With Fractions

The shapes below are split into parts, or fractions. Color only the shapes that are split into equal parts (equal fractions).

1.

2.

3.

4.

5.

6.

7.

8.

Parts to Color

Color $\frac{1}{5}$ of the circle.

A **fraction** has two numbers. The top number will tell you how many parts to color. The bottom number tells you how many parts there are.

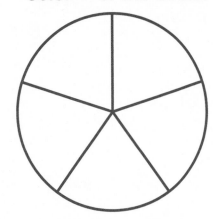

Color $\frac{4}{5}$ of the rectangle.

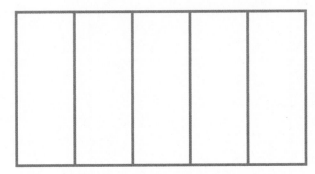

Color $\frac{3}{5}$ of the ants.

Color $\frac{2}{5}$ of the spiders.

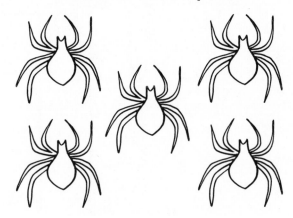

Color $\frac{0}{5}$ of the bees.

Color $\frac{5}{5}$ of the worms.

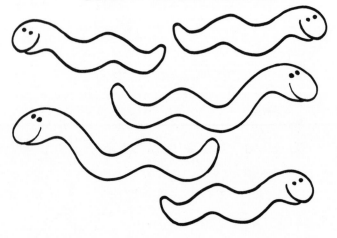

More Parts to Color

Color $\frac{1}{8}$ of the circle.

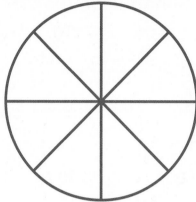

Color $\frac{6}{8}$ of the rectangle.

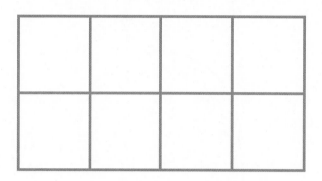

Color $\frac{4}{8}$ of the suns.

Color $\frac{8}{8}$ of the stars.

Color $\frac{2}{8}$ of the moons.

Color $\frac{3}{8}$ of the planets.

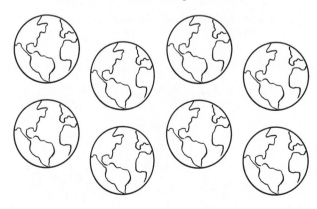

Clock Work

Draw the hands on the clock so it shows **2:00**.

Draw the hands on the clock so it shows **7:00**.

Draw the hands on the clock so it shows **4:00**.

Draw the hands on the clock so it shows **5:00**.

What do you do at 2:00 in the afternoon?
Write about it on the lines below.

_____

_____

More Clock Work

Draw the hands on the clock so it shows **3:00**.

Draw the hands on the clock so it shows **6:00**.

Draw the hands on the clock so it shows **9:00**.

Draw the hands on the clock so it shows **12:00**.

What do you do at 3:00 in the afternoon?
Write about it on the lines below.

_____

_____

Even More Clock Work

Draw the hands on the clock so it shows **1:00**.

Draw the hands on the clock so it shows **4:30**.

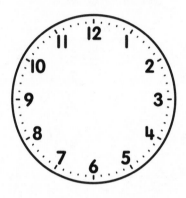

What do you do at 4:00 in the afternoon? Write about it on the line below.

_____

Draw the hands on the clock so it shows **8:00**.

Draw the hands on the clock so it shows **6:30**.

What do you do at 8:00 in the evening? Write about it on the line below.

_____

About Time

Why do we need to know how to tell time? List your ideas below.

_____

_____

_____

_____

How long is a minute?

Think about how much you can do in one minute.
Write your estimates in the Prediction column.
Then time yourself. Write the actual number
in the Result column.

Prediction: In one minute I can...	Result
jump rope _____ times.	
write the numbers 1 to _____.	
say the names of _____ animals.	

ANSWER KEY

Page 5
4 tens 7 ones, 6 tens 4 ones;
7 tens 8 ones, 9 tens 6 ones

Page 6
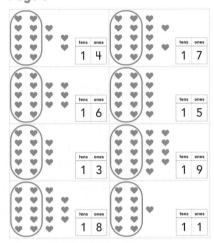

Page 7
Yield sign: triangle, 3
Caution sign: diamond, 4
Speed-limit sign: rectangle, 4
Stop sign: octagon, 8

Page 8
Left bird feeder: cube, octagon, hexagon, rectangle, square, rectangle solid
Right bird feeder: cylinder, triangle, circle, rectangle

Page 9
Color the first butterfly, the second heart, the light bulb, and the snowflake.
Drawings should show the other halves.

Page 10
Drawings should show the other half of each shape.

Page 11
1. 32, 42, 52, 62, 72, 82, 92
2. 70, 60, 50, 40, 30, 20, 10
3. 67, 57, 47, 37, 27, 17, 7
4. 44, 55, 66, 77, 88, 99

Page 12
Possible answers:
2. This is a pattern of three shapes, each a different color, that repeat.
3. This is a pattern of three. All three are the same shape but are colored differently.
4. This is a pattern of sets of three numbers. The pattern continues by adding 1 to each of the three numbers.

Page 13
1. Answers will vary.
2. Numbers will be colored in using an AB pattern of red and blue.

Page 14
Estimates will vary. 2, 4, 6, 8, 10, 12, 14, 16, 18, 20; 5, 10, 15, 20

Page 15

1	2	3	4	5	6	7	8	9	10
11	12	13	14	15	16	17	18	19	20
21	22	23	24	25	26	27	28	29	30
31	32	33	34	35	36	37	38	39	40
41	42	43	44	45	46	47	48	49	50
51	52	53	54	55	56	57	58	59	60
61	62	63	64	65	66	67	68	69	70
71	72	73	74	75	76	77	78	79	80
81	82	83	84	85	86	87	88	89	90
91	92	93	94	95	96	97	98	99	100

Answers will vary.

Page 16
Patterns and equations will vary.

Page 17
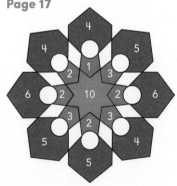

Page 18
6 + 2 = 8, 4 + 3 = 7, 2 + 1 = 3,
4 + 1 = 5, 11 + 3 = 14, 8 + 2 = 10,
7 + 5 = 12, 9 + 2 = 11, 6 + 3 = 9,
11 + 4 = 15, 5 + 13 = 18, 9 + 4 = 13
A PIANO

Page 19
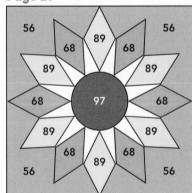

	17	36	84	
78	29	59	14	48
88	24	35	66	98
18	43	77	38	88
78	65	56	46	26
	99	57	87	

Page 20
93 + 6 = 99, 82 + 4 = 86, 14 + 5 = 19,
21 + 7 = 28, 53 + 6 = 59,
45 + 4 = 49, 73 + 3 = 76, 36 + 3 = 39,
61 + 5 = 66, 32 + 7 = 39

Page 21
A flower diagram with numbers: 56 in each corner, 89 on outer petals, 68 on inner petals, and 97 in the center.

Page 22

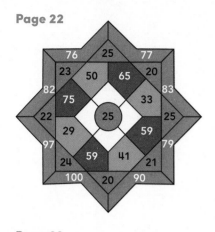

Page 23

four, five; seven, eleven; nine, six; ten, three; eight, two

f	o	u	r	h	i	o	n	e	g	s	k	m
i	f	o	n	t	g	y	f	a	f	u	e	z
f	t	l	u	e	j	s	i	x	s	b	x	l
t	t	w	e	l	v	e	v	k	s	t	t	h
e	p	n	i	n	e	w	e	j	e	r	l	i
e	d	n	g	q	i	h	r	y	v	a	q	r
n	v	h	h	o	t	h	r	e	e	c	s	t
d	m	k	t	c	w	b	t	e	n	t	r	e
x	d	i	p	g	o	a	c	p	f	i	s	e
c	e	l	e	v	e	n	a	b	z	o	v	n
b	w	u	d	i	f	f	e	r	e	n	c	e

Pages 24–25

1. 10 − 3 = 7   **2.** 6 − 4 = 2
3. 10 − 1 = 9   **4.** 8 − 7 = 1
5. 4 − 1 = 3   **6.** 10 − 4 = 6
7. 10 − 6 = 4   **8.** 10 − 8 = 2
9. 7 − 4 = 3

Page 26

2, 4, 2; 3, 6, 4; 6, 4, 10

Page 27

34 + 13 = 47, 21 + 52 = 73,
47 + 10 = 57, 75 − 34 = 41,
62 − 21 = 41, 47 − 13 = 34

Page 28

38 + 24 = 62, 50 + 49 = 99,
56 + 25 = 81;
72 − 49 = 23, 56 − 24 = 32,
50 − 25 = 25

Page 29

Answers will vary.

Page 30

3 1/2 inches, 2 inches,
1 1/2 inches, 3 inches
Patty, Peter, Petunia, Paul

Page 31

pencil: 2   **lunch box:** 1
crayon: 2   **notebook:** 1

Page 32

1 gallon = 4 quarts
1 quart = 2 pints
1 pint = 2 cups
1 cup = 12 tablespoons
1 tablespoon = 3 teaspoons

Page 33

book width: 2 centimeters
paper height: 3 centimeters
key: 4 centimeters
brush: 6 centimeters
5 cubes: 4 centimeters
10 cubes: 8 centimeters
shoe: 5 centimeters
hand: 3 centimeters

Page 34

Answers may vary. Check graph to make sure that it corresponds to the boxes checked.
chicken: see, hear, smell, touch
sun: see
milk: see, touch, taste
flowers: see, smell, touch
drums: see, hear, touch

Page 35

Answers will vary.

Page 36

2. (F, 6)   **3.** (H, 10)   **4.** (D, 1)
5. (E, 8)   **6.** (C, 4)   **7.** (I, 5)
8. (G, 3)   **9.** (A, 7)   **10.** (J, 2)

Page 37

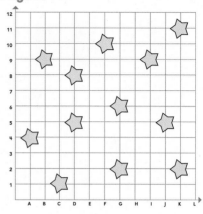

Page 38

Sunny days: 12
Cloudy days: 8
Rainy days: 5
Snowy days: 6
Sunny days

Page 39

Color shapes 1, 2, 5, 6, 7, and 8.

Page 40

Page 41

Page 42

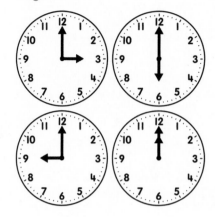

Page 43

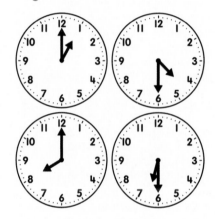

Page 44

Page 45
Answers will vary.